A Daughter for Mr. Spider

Megan Russo

Published by Nightingale & Sparrow Press, 2020

Copyright © 2020 Megan Russo

All rights reserved. This book or any portion thereof may not be reproduced or used in any manner whatsoever without the express written permission of the publisher except for the use of brief quotations in a book review.

ISBN: 9781694148094

For Paul Edward

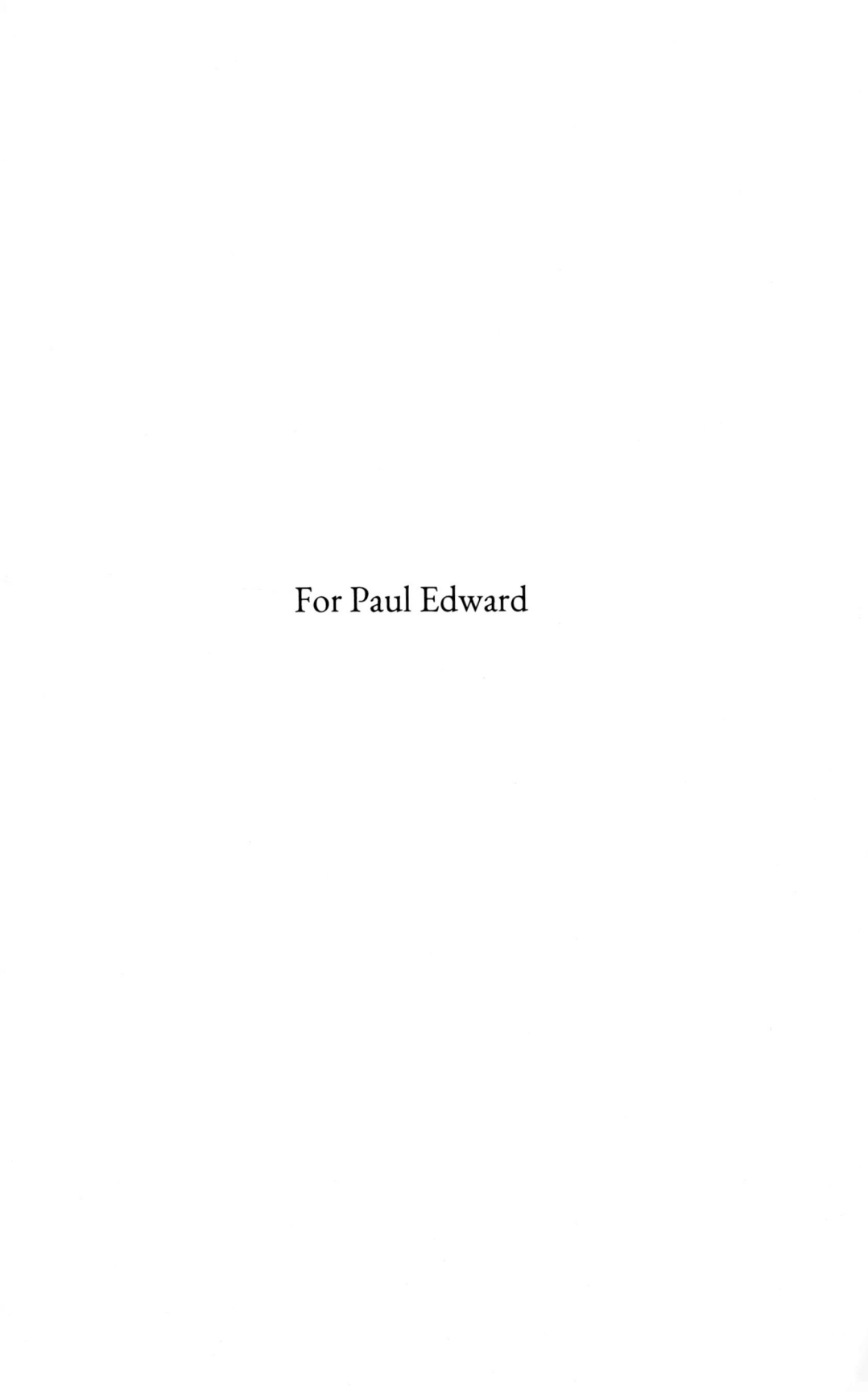

A Daughter for Mr. Spider

father

My father's name was David, and he was good at math.

He liked motorcycles and dog racing. He was a boisterous man with good teeth and a full head of ashy blond hair. He collected shot glasses from places, nowhere special. A sequence in time that he memorialized on a handmade display rack in the basement of tan colored ranch house that he rented from his uncle. He collected other things: VHS tapes, pocket knives, interesting rocks, and stolen bank pens with the silver ball chains still attached.

He was a white trash hero, bragging about finally fixing the car that had been parked in his front yard for the past four months. He had driven it around the block once before parking in back where it had previously dwelled. It had served its purpose.

David had gone to night school instead of a four year college. His brother eventually helped him find a decent job as a finance manager at a used car lot; Liberty Auto Jeep, Dodge, and Chrysler. It was a place where a cabal of slick-palmed white men gathered every day until 9:00PM. Grumbling and snickering while tethering balloons to side-view mirrors and untangling nests of crepe paper ribbons from the prickly fabric walls of private cubicles.

They were a hive mind only loosely controlled in their aimlessness, pacing the polished floor and whispering curses under their breath as they waited for lunch time, then closing time. They all wore matching ties, only fresh once a week when the cheap polyester pieces were picked from the dry cleaner down the street. At night they were left behind in a box in the break room. A crumbled mess next to a garbage can filled with soggy coffee filters and candy wrappers.

David had an office, and with a receptionist.

My mother.

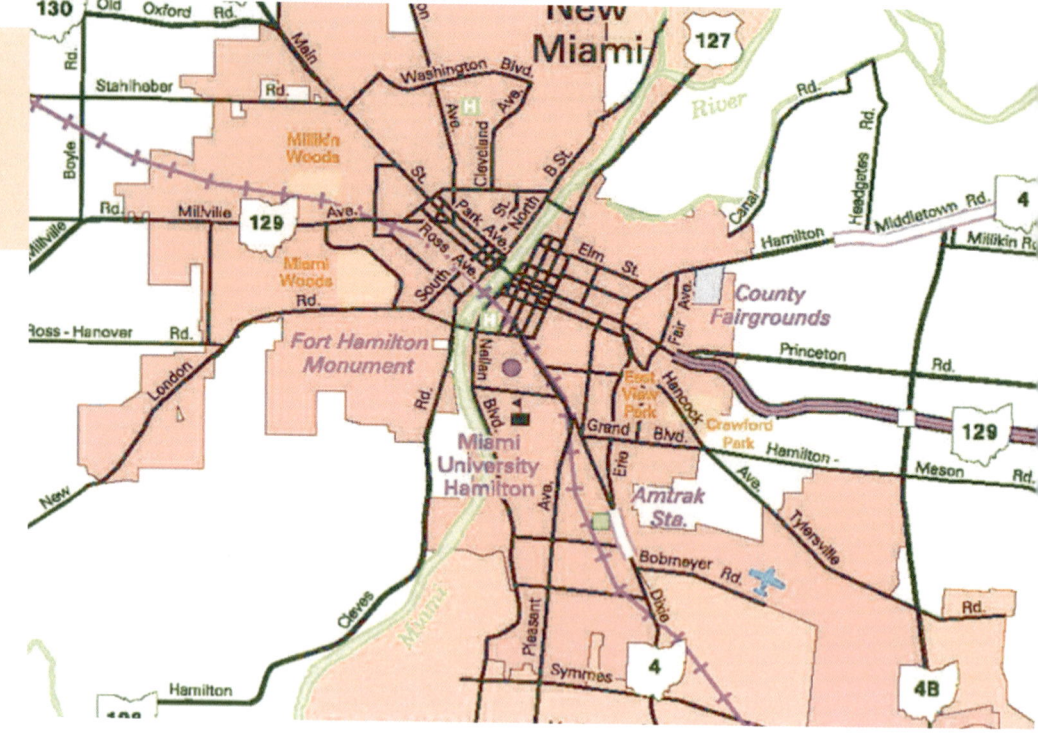

You are a true romantic as you
wine and dine me with your *real* leather wallet.
Take me out to one of the nicer places,
give me freedom from my parents,
and for just these moments,
you feel like treating me right.
We hit up the gas station on the way back to your place
chug a few wine coolers on the drive.
While Poison barely plays through static country air,
I tell you that I love you, and you say that sounds good.
We do it.
Then it's over.
Vanishing romance as the second hand ticks.
We are nothing.

To whom it may concern:

Please accept this letter as notice that I will be resigning from my job here at Liberty Auto Jeep, Dodge, and Chrysler two weeks from today's date.

Thank you for the support and the opportunities you have provided me over the course of the last six months. You and our team have created a climate that makes it a pleasure to come to work each morning, and I will miss you all.

If I can do anything to help with your transition in finding and training my replacement, please let me know.

Sincerely,

Mother

Goodbye, David.

You were a scum lover.

Maybe we've met
staring at the same box of cereal
or rushing to the produce section to find the perfect orange.
I'd stab you in the heart with a sharpened asparagus.
She wanted to hold you close
wrapped in her embrace and gentled by her touch
comforted by your scent
the dollar store laundry detergent.
She wanted to brush your tangled hair
bury her fingers deeper and deeper into the unkempt nest
chase away the strands as they catch in your eyelashes
you hated when she called them pretty.
She didn't care that you were older
you weren't a conquest to her
just a meaningful connection
but you weren't truly interested.

You fucked up, Father.
Can I even call you that?

mother

She hated the way her name was spelled. All the other girls spelled it with an EY or and IE, but she had been stuck with a flawed version of what could have been the *perfect* name. Stacy. It was a popular name back then, and she was just one of a dozen girls in her high school with the name, but none spelled it wrong like her.

My mother was a jock. Volleyball, soccer, softball. Two rules, play it or cheer for it as loud as she could in the wooden bleachers of her high school. If there was a club she would join it. She wanted to be involved, wanted to be seen and noticed by those around her.

This youngest child would not be ignored. She would be the best one.

The best sister. The best daughter.

She had aways hated being stagnant, needing to be needed by those around her. A provider. A shoulder to cry on when your boyfriend dumped you or the manager at your part time job made a pass at you. She was Stacy with no E, and at that time she wanted to be wanted.

She couldn't imagine a time where she would want to go unnoticed.

so full of promise.

1988

You were beautiful and cocky as you drove around in your red Ford Escort. You ran your electric purple fingernails through your dark curls while shouting the lyrics to Darling Nikki and smacking the steering wheel each time Prince sang the word *grind*. Your friend Julie rode shotgun, pouting in the flip-down mirror as she applied another layer of sticky peach lip gloss that made the whole car smell heavenly until you cranked the window down. All the while your best friend Lyle sulked, perturbed that he had been chosen to climb into the backseat. You had rolled your eyes when he let out a pained groan as he found himself ankle deep in grease soaked fast food wrappers and crushed soda cans. His car was more of a piece of shit than yours was. You sucked down another luke warm can of Mountain Dew since volleyball season was finally over and your freedom had been officially restored.

Big hair and icy grey eyes. A sporty goddess born in 1972, sweat pants and pristine white sneakers.

The youngest of 4. Carla, Beverly, Geri Lynn, and Stacy. I was the funny one and they were just the set dressing. I hadn't been looking for love when I met David, but I thought that just maybe something nice could come out of it. Something more than just another friendship. Not another casual banishment to the friend zone since I wasn't a size 2 with large breasts. I liked to go out and do things. I'm not like all the other Stacies. I have so much more to offer. But whatever. If he doesn't like me then I could surely find someone else. There are tons of guys out there and while not all of them are my type, there has to be one. Or maybe I'll just travel after college and find myself. A real deal boyfriend isn't something that you have to have. You can just be your own person and be happy knowing that you are living the life you've chosen. We are not defined by another and that should feel like an accomplishment, right? Well maybe not, because having someone to share everything with would be nice and maybe if we went out to dinner, David would see me as something more. I can be adult and I can him over with my charm, and I'm fucking funny for christ sake. He loves my jokes and personality is really the foundation of a good relationship in my opinion. Just maybe this could work out. But you never know until you give it a try, right? That's what they say. Plus free dinner would be pretty nice.

the beginning of the end.

1991

Maybe you were putting on weight because you had been studying so hard and were using sugar as late night fuel...but we know that wasn't the case.

I arrived in January, not the best gift to begin a new year, but still I came. You were a senior in high school who had scored a 33 on your ACT and had spent months planning on what college you wanted to attend. You had a goal that you had been working toward since you worked your first summer at the YMCA as a life guard and swim instructor, saving all the money you made to get an apartment after graduation. You had put in your time teaching snarky senior citizens water aerobics with chlorine-soaked spongy barbells at 7:30 AM on Saturdays, and where was that going to get you now?

You had thought I was just a bad dream, but as the days went by, you knew the truth. There was no way this was happening to you, because you were one of the smart ones. You had a future and then it was gone. Everything swallowed up by round black eyes that studied you in ways that made your skin cold.

A spider's eyes.

How can I ruin your future today?

Our history
is an open wound on the palm of my hand.
Infection settling in the mangled flesh,
claiming territory as its own,
a mottled landscape of silenced anger
and bared teeth.
My hands wrapped around my neck,
nails cutting in—
the corners of my vision black
as I try to punish myself.
Torment and agony are what I deserve
for taking everything,
stealing it all away from you.
I had eaten your dreams,
gnashing and cruelly smirking,
while you were in pain—
and I knew.
I felt the coldness there—
silence between us,
when I called your name.
Mommy.
Mother.
Stacy.

I was an unfeeling spirit trapped in an infant's body.

A demon that had clawed its way out

from another universe

hellbent on tearing you apart

and bringing ruin to you.

They said I was lovely,

but you knew what I was,

a haunted doll that refused to sleep,

eyes open,

and searching in the void.

I saw through you,

deep inside the uncertainty of your presence.

I could sense your fear,

the anger you feel toward yourself,

because you weren't a failure.

Yet,

you didn't know what to do with me.

So you left me by his pit

and hoped he would take pity.

An old spider hopefully willing to

help raise another creature of solitude.

Show me his ways,

and stop me from becoming a beast.

can you even forgive me now?

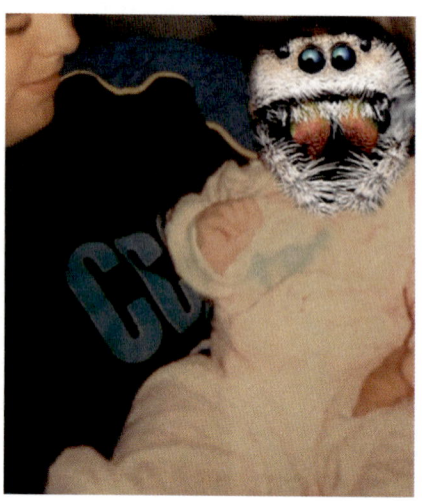

*can you forgive me for what
I took away?*

mr. spider

Mr. Spider was a cautious caregiver filled with the wisdom of many years on earth. He had raised many children before me, but claimed I would be his last. He had rules by which he lived his life, a creature of habit to the bitter end.

I was carried in his arms wherever we went, lifted high onto his back with ease. I traveled above the land, out of the grasp of the creatures that surrounded us, and lived among the stars.

Pay them no mind, they mean nothing to those like us.

Mr. Spider hurried quickly to our destinations. Always taking me with him, never leaving me behind. Always early.

We respect the time of others, and hope they do the same for us.

His coloring was red, grey and white, shades that still catch my eye when I see others like him out in the world. He smelled like steel and sweet potatoes. He loved reading yellowed paperbacks about cowboys and aimless drifters. A lifestyle that maybe he had once considered, but knew it wasn't practical for him.

He was a stranger to the wealthy city men, but a lord amongst those who kept to the shadows to do their honest work. He made sure I never wanted for anything. He was always quick to respond, so quiet in his love. There was a barrier around him, an obsidian shield that protected his emotions, but when he held me close enough I could feel them there. I could hear his heart beating, and it helped me to hear my own.

He was 1 of 13 siblings, never sharing much about his childhood. Others we met would often tell tales of his youth, tricks and sly cons he ran. Some claimed the wealthy city men howled like a pack of wild dogs when Mr. Spider was done with them. He could make those fools go mad. But then they claimed that was all in the past and Mr. Spider didn't protest.

You're an old man now, Mr. Spider.

But I could see there was still a glimmer of the old trickery in the black depth of his eyes; eyes that were so familiar to my own that I found comforting in ways I couldn't explain.

He cackled at the way I would clumsily hug his face, chelicerae twitching with affection as my arms were unable to encircle his massive form. A sloppy child's kiss. He smiled when I'd lie face down on the floor covered in one of his old blankets. The scent of the fabric was calming to my restless spirit. I would pretend to be a rug, slowly creeping closer to him as if he would be surprised by my approach. I did this often, sometimes multiple times a day, but he would always act surprised when I jumped up to try and scare him.

Why a rug, little spider?

i think i just want to be a rug when i grow up

I'm glad to see you have goals, my dear.

As a child I loved Mr. Spider more than I had ever loved another. He was my universe. He was monumental, the top of my head barely reaching the middle of his legs when I stood next to him. It would only be a few seconds before he'd scoop me up once more, tossing me on his back again. My fingers would tangle in his black hair, but he never seemed to mind the scratching of my short baby nails.

Hold tight to me.

At night he'd sink away into the darkness, off to do his work as I slept, but always there when I would wake. It was as if he never slept, just curled up in the back of his web, waiting for me to need him.

The day light hours were my hours for learning, and Mr. Spider was a teacher of many arts. Gardening, reading, popular television viewing, but writing was his favorite. With a steadiness he taught me to write, starting with my last name. It was most important to him.

They will know you are one of mine.

They will want to know your name one day.

You need to be ready to share it.

He was jovial when I decided to get married. He wore a white rose on his tuxedo and danced with me to our favorite Johnny Cash song while the creatures in attendance slugged drink after drink to drown out their own worries on my joyous day. My husband laughed as he waited for his chance to dance alongside his mother. As we took our final bow, I hugged Mr. Spider tightly. I had never seen him so happy.

Take good care of my daughter, Timothy.

Softness
emotions that I can finally see
did it take me leaving for you to feel open
no
I shouldn't think that way
you have found a happiness within my own
a moment
seconds in time that we will always have
the minutes we share together.

He didn't tell me he was dying. He never said the word. I heard it second hand from the others. He didn't want to upset me. He didn't know if this was really his fate. However, we went through it together. I cried every night. Too afraid to speak to him at times, because he held himself together so well and I was a disaster. We tried treatments. Horrible things that made him sick and miserable, but he wanted to live. He wanted another chance. There was a desperation that I saw for a single fraction of a second.

Then it was gone.

Maybe he was just as terrified as I was, but then he decided it was over.

When Mr. Spider died I was there. I watched his eyes flutter and skin begin to lose all color. I help his hand tightly until they pulled me away. I needed to leave. They wanted to try. They wanted to save him, but then they failed.

I pounded my fists against my thighs. I was angry. I was filled with a hatred that spewed from my mouth and coated my world in acid. It crumbled around me. Buildings sinking to their knees as I snarled and shrieked. My eyes were wide with fury as I blamed them all. You failed. You failed to save him and I hate you with every fiber of my being.

He's dead. Mr. Spider is dead.

WHY?

Why did you have to die?

I've been cursed,

stricken with a malady.

I have his eyes.

A reflection that cackles at me

each time I have the misfortune of meeting the gaze of a mirror.

Endlessness that calls me back to him.

When I see myself,

I am consumed by the depths,

the memories attached to immovable orbs.

The infinite holes draw me in.

We shared this darkness,

until—

then it was just me.

The one left burning bright.

Doomed to repetition.

Bound to keep him close and swirling within me.

We shall not meet face to face,
wandering in this trance,
and my sanity rippling at the edges.
The doctors promised me that
I won't feel hundreds of gleaming teeth
reach for me through the dark,
tearing at my paper skin,
but how could they know how persistent you are?
My screams muted by medications
and disapproving glances.
Vignetted visions of your face
that I won't soon forget.
I float into my medicated horizon,
and wait to sleep again.

i will always hum that song you like
i want you to need me
give me purpose again.

I sympathize with impulse,

embarrassingly recalling my most recent

breakdown on that Saturday in June.

I had taken every framed photo of him off the walls of my apartment,

deciding that it would be better if they were

tucked away in my closet.

I was convinced that this new apartment was not mine

and it would never be mine.

He had never seen the place.

Never given his approval.

Why try to make it feel like my home?

Why had I wasted my valuable time trying to claim something

that I could never really have?

Why did I even keep so much stupid shit like this anyway?

I tucked my chin into my chest,

being deliberate with my breathing in the strange

way I found comforting,

as my mind told me what it wanted me to do.

Just leave.

Leave everything behind and find him.

He wasn't really dead.

They had just told me that so that they could take him away from me.

I wasn't allowed to go, but I could see him vividly as my hands twitched.

Had I really strayed this far?

So I decided to return

I had to see it for myself again

days

weeks

endless seconds flying by with each breath

trembling

inescapable

a pull that brought me back to that place

the once upturned earth

now just one of many

another grave

overgrown with vicious nature

couldn't read the words

fingers running over the carved stone

mouthing along with the syllables

trying to feel you there

but

you're still gone

maybe you weren't so special after all.

now what?

[overlapping text: I don't know / I didn't think I'd live this / what I was trying to / why am I still trying to / a fight I was trying to / right. How can I keep / doing this? I keep]

I need to move forward. That is what he taught me. That is what he would have wanted. He would have felt so much pain to see the mess I had become.

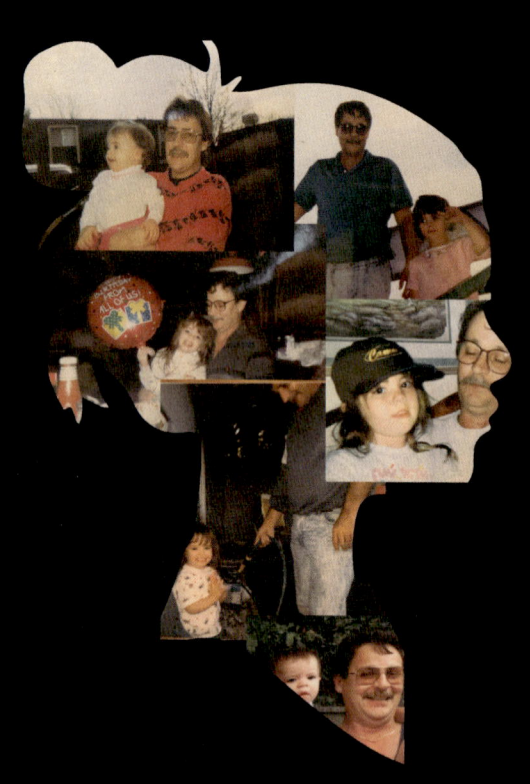

..., passed awa,
  .1 Cincinnati on November 4.
  /iami. Paul worked at AK Stee
  .ly, and even though he worked i.
  cowboy at heart. He loved workin<
  'ng, taking care of animals, and Joh
  .vas a great husband, father, and fri
  aul was blessed to come from a large
  lition he continued when starting
  led in death by his parents Hen
  ll as brothers and sister Elizab(
  'n. Paul is survived by his wife F
  'en, great-grandchild, b1
  and in-laws that was buii.
  '. care of all of us. So we are
  .n. Visitation will be held on V

Mother: "I've heard that people who have that disorder don't do the things you do. It doesn't make sense."

spider spawn: "what doesn't make sense?"

Mother: "Anything you do."

spider spawn: "well I've started the process of seeing someone, and maybe they will have some answers for me."

Mother: "I'm hopeful."

spider spawn: "yep."

Learn to forgive
and dress the wounds of self harm.
Cast away those thoughts,
that are sharp like daggers,
memories more crippling
than physical pain.
Yet, now we have arrived
a place to lay everything out.
Carefully lining up baggage you've drug behind you.
You have reached your destination.
Time to unpack and then pack,
just to finally unpack again.
There's no right grieving order,
as old scars pile up,
preserved so neatly in your suitcase.
Yet as you look at them now,
they have closed,
building material,
for a stairway to somewhere,
a new place.
Stand upon the first step,
and

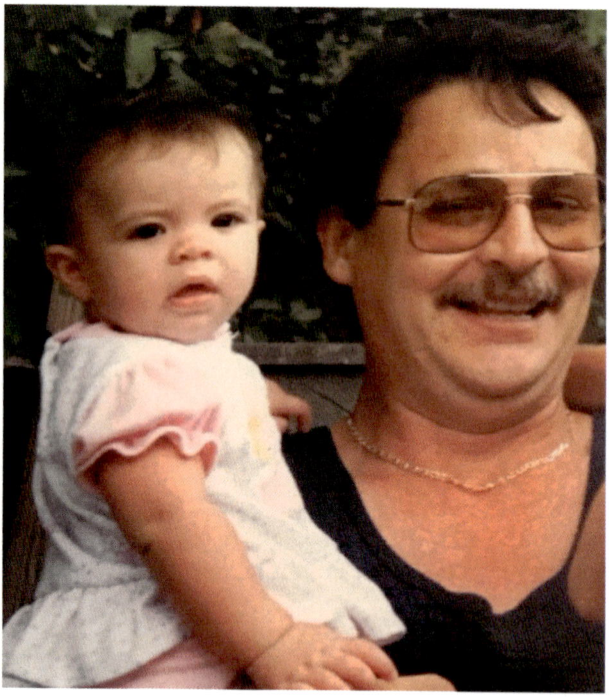

I keep your memories in a box on my nightstand, the top closed tightly to make sure they stay safe inside. As a child I had watched you build it, carefully measuring and constructing. Until one day it was just there, a wooden chest that fit in your hand, both of mine at that age.

It is a thing of wonder.

You told me I would build my own one day, but that time was far in the distance. I watched you fill it through the years, bits and pieces of you tucked away. Saving them, passing them down to me before your death. Ensuring I still had you, and was never alone.

I open it every night, letting your memories dance through my own. Always a joyful reunion, finding each other in the shared history we have. It feels like waking, all of this has been the dream and I've awoken once more to see your face. To hear you say my name again. I cannot forget your voice.

There she is, my daughter.

My Megan.

Good night, Mr. Spider.

until we wake again.

About the Author

Megan is a writer and graphic designer living in Austin, TX. Her work has been published by *Palm Sized Press, Cauldron Anthology, Royal Rose Magazine, Wellington Street Review*, among others. When she's not playing tabletop games or spreading the gospel of her devotion to pastel color schemes, she enjoys seeing live shows around the city and spending time with her husband and their two pugs.

Find her at meganrusso.com or @forgewithstyle on Twitter or Instagram.

If you enjoyed *A Daughter for Mr. Spider*....

Consider leaving a review on Amazon, Goodreads, or your favourite website (or tell a friend!).

Recommend or donate a copy to your local library.

Try one of our previously published titles or an issue of our literary magazine and stay tuned for these upcoming publications from Nightingale & Sparrow Press:

Natalie by Keana Aguila Labra (May 2020)

you were supposed to be a friend by Ashley Elizabeth (June 2020)

Bouquet of Fears by Noa Covo (July 2020)

All the Shades of Grief by Ellora Sutton (September 2020)

Queer Girl Falls by Lannie Stabile (September 2020)

Heal My Way Home by Rachel Tanner (October 2020)

ephemeral by Samantha Rose (November 2020)

What Lasts Beyond the Burning by A.A. Parr (December 2020)

Keep up to date with *Nightingale & Sparrow*:

nightingaleandsparrow.com

Facebook: /nightingaleandsparrow

Twitter: @nightandsparrow

Instagram: @nightingaleandsparrow

Made in the USA
Columbia, SC
25 May 2020